THE

Soul

CHALLENGE

What a Difference One Year Can Make

Rickey Rambo

THE SOUL CHALLENGE

What a Difference One Year Can Make

Copyright©2023 by Rickey Rambo

Critical Mass Books

Haymarket, Virginia

www.criticalmasspublishing.com

1st Edition

ISBN: 978-1-947153-40-0

| Cover Design | Eowyn Riggins |
| Interior Layout | Rachel Newhouse |

Dedication

To my wonderful and lovely wife Keshawn, who challenges herself to be a godly woman, which challenges me to be a godly man. To my awesome son Devin, who challenges everybody to be givers, which challenges me to keep giving to others. To my wonderful daughter Chelsea who challenges herself to be a phenomenal and godly young lady who excels in all she does and inspires me in my ministry journey. I dedicate this book to you. And to my parents, my family, and Sunlight, thank you for allowing me to be your pastor and always encouraging me.

Contents

ONE

"The Challenge"

I feel a lot like the Prophet Jeremiah when God took him down to the Potter's House. God has worked on my heart, which I have yielded to Him as clay for His mighty hands. He has molded a message deep inside me, and He has shown me some exciting things that He wants me to share far and wide.

They have to do with vision—not just for the short term, but for the long haul. We live in the day of 24/7 news and things that capture our attention one day seemed to drift out of our minds by the next day. It's the age of soundbites and *Twitter*. We prefer short phrases, some not very well thought through, to anything lengthier. It's almost like the whole world has *Attention Deficit Disorder*.

Certainly, it appears that the church does in many ways.

But for us to truly and fully yield to the King of Kings, and to be His devoted followers, we must be willing not only to invest the time, we must also start thinking in terms of years rather than mere minutes or hours. And I think that is exactly why God has put it on my heart to tell you about what I call *The One-Year Soul Challenge*.

Yes—one whole year.

As we get started, I'd like you to find a picture of yourself from at least a decade ago.

Then I want you to place that picture right beside one taken recently. If you're like me, you'll notice quite a change. Maybe your weight is different or your hair color or style has changed some. There is no way the pictures will look exactly the same, even if you use the same pose and background.

Now, using your imagination and try to picture what you might look like ten years from now. Let's take this idea further by focusing not on external appearances, but rather on internal realities. Things like spiritual growth, character, Christ-likeness—how will these things compare in ten years to where you are right now?

The fact is that our flesh will change, and there's nothing we can really do about it. Facelifts, diets, Botox, injections on parts of our bodies, muscle pills, and such things won't, in the long-run, make a bit of difference. We can nip and tuck all we want, but like some kind of gravitational pull, our bodies are going to decline.

No matter how much energy or money you invest searching for some magic pill or fountain of youth, we know from the first pages of the Bible, "*In the sweat of thy face shalt thou eat bread, till thou return unto the ground; for out of it wast thou taken: for dust thou art, and unto dust shalt thou return.*"[1]

The Bible is clear that we should guard against comparing ourselves with others: "*For we dare not make ourselves of the number, or **compare** ourselves with some that commend themselves: but they measuring themselves by themselves, and comparing themselves among themselves, are not wise.*"[2] But comparing ourselves with ourselves is an entirely different matter. And what I want to show you is how to compare your "now" with your "later"—particularly one year later.

That's the goal of this One-Year Challenge.

This is a soul challenge. God wants us to be intentional about our soul. He wants us to partner with Him in our sanctification process. He never wants us to be haphazard about our spiritual growth. And this is why we need *soul goals*. These are quite different from earthly or fleshly goals—what the Bible calls *carnal*.

The best example of carnal goals is probably what we do in New Year's Resolutions.

They tend to be all about our flesh. We want more money. We want a promotion on the job—or maybe a better place to work. Possibly, a new car that year is the goal. Soul goals, however, are very different. They are about putting God and His Kingdom first!

In other words, we're talking about *sanctification*.

Sanctification is one of those wonderful Bible terms we need to understand more than we do. It is something that impacts the wholeness of the person. It means to be "set apart" by God so He can complete what is lacking in us. It's both a process and a goal. This is what the Apostle Paul was talking about in his letter to the church at Philippi:

> "...being confident of this very thing, that He who has begun a good work in you will complete it until the day of Jesus Christ;"
>
> —PHILIPPIANS 1:6 (NKJV)

What was it that gave Paul such confidence? It was simply this; *"that very thing..."*— which was that their longevity was of God. He started it; He was in it; and He would finish it. His exhortation to yet another church was:

"Be ye steadfast, unmovable always abounding in the work of the Lord, forasmuch as ye know that your labor is not in vain in the Lord."

—I Corinthians 15:58 (KJV)

Just as, in the earthly or physical realm, a baby naturally grows toward adulthood, so a believer should supernaturally grow toward spiritual maturity. That means the likeness or image of Jesus Christ. The same Apostle expanded on this in his letter to the believers at Rome:

"And we know that all things work together for good to those who love God, to those who are the called according to His purpose. For whom He foreknew, He also predestined to be conformed to the image of His Son, that He might be the firstborn among many brethren."

— Romans 8:28-29 (NKJV)

Becoming increasingly conformed to the image of Christ culminates in complete sanctification, allowing us to be the best version of ourselves. It means that we can be godly in every sense of the word. God wants us to be intentional about this. That's where soul goals come in. He wants us to partner with Him in the sanctification process. There is no room for haphazardness when it comes to true spirituality.

We must focus like a laser beam on what God wants and has for us. And this means every move needs to be a faith move. Why? Because it goes against every part of our human nature. It all seems so illogical to focus on the unseen over what we see.

TWO

"The Catalyst"

*"Therefore do not worry, saying, 'What shall we eat?' or
'What shall we drink?' or 'What shall we wear?' For after all
these things the Gentiles seek. For your heavenly Father
knows that you need all these things. But seek first the
kingdom of God and His righteousness, and all these things
shall be added to you."*

—MATTHEW 6:33 (KJV)

In His famous Sermon on the Mount, Jesus shared what has
been described as The Manifesto of the Kingdom. It is the
basis of all of the subsequent teachings of the New Testament
as found in the doctrinal and practical books which follow the
Acts of the Apostles to the book of Revelation.

To understand this is to unlock the door of biblical
revelation and spiritual understanding, especially as it relates

to the age in which we now live. Jesus describes a life of faith and faithfulness, one that flows from a relationship with Him.

In this relationship the believer fully realizes with complete understanding that *"our God will supply all our need according to his riches in glory by Christ Jesus". (Phil. 4:19)* Therefore, just as a child has complete trust in his earthly father to supply all his needs so Christians need never worry about things in this world. The Just shall live by faith, and faith is confidence which leads to trust that in turn results in commitment to grow spiritually. In fact:

> *"Without faith it is impossible to please Him, for he that cometh to God must believe that He is, and that he is a rewarder of those who diligently seek Him."*
>
> —HEBREWS 11:6 (NKJV)

Illustration after illustration is given by our Lord to enforce this truth. The birds of the air; the lilies of the field etc., all show that it is the Heavenly Father who is not only aware of everything but also in control of everything.

Just as it is true that we cannot affect our physical growth and do not worry about it, so also we are to trust the Lord for everything in life.

The key is to seek first, in our lives, the kingdom of God and then simply believe that the Father will provide our needs. Do not worry about what will happen tomorrow; make sure to live pleasing the Lord today.

To seek the kingdom of God of course refers to man's basic need of personal salvation. The kingdom of God is spiritual not physical. It is entered by way of the New Birth where we are Born Again "from above."

Another way of saying *"seek first the Kingdom of God,"* would be: Seek His sanctification goals (soul goals) for your Life. The way we do this is by embracing and delighting in Him and in His purposes for our lives.

> *"Delight yourself also in the Lord,*
> *And He shall give you the desires of your heart."*
> —PSALM 37:4 (NKJV)

If we seek Him first and delight in Him, He will fulfill our godly desires. In a real sense, God will work on our "tastes." He wants to change our emotional taste buds so our desires line up with His.

That's a large part of sanctification.

God has given us the ultimate tool to help us with sanctification—His Word.

"Therefore lay aside all filthiness and [d]overflow of wickedness, and receive with meekness the implanted word, which is able to save your souls. But be doers of the word, and not hearers only, deceiving yourselves. For if anyone is a hearer of the word and not a doer, he is like a man observing his natural face in a mirror; for he observes himself, goes away, and immediately forgets what kind of man he was. But he who looks into the perfect law of liberty and continues in it, and is not a forgetful hearer but a doer of the work, this one will be blessed in what he does."

—JAMES 1:21-25 (NKJV)

Notice that it says the Word is "implanted" in us. In other words, it's an agent of salvation. It acts as a catalyst working in us for regeneration (another word for salvation). You have a "catalytic converter" in your car. In simple terms, this device removes harmful gases from your vehicle's exhaust, cleaning it so it can operate properly. It's the same principle with the Word in our hearts and minds. The Word removes what is harmful in our lives so we can grow properly.

In First Peter 1:23, we learn that we are *"born again, not of corruptible seed but incorruptible,* **through the word of God** *which lives and abides forever."* And we know from the Romans 1:17 that, *"faith comes by hearing. and hearing by the Word of God."*

The Word and sanctification are a life-changing team. We need to dedicate ourselves to hearing the Word, reading the Word, and believing the Word. So, any plan for a better life (soul growth) begins with a re-commitment to the Word of God.

On His way to the cross, Jesus told His disciples:

"I am the true vine, and My Father is the vinedresser. Every branch in Me that does not bear fruit He takes away; and every branch that bears fruit He prunes, that it may bear more fruit. You are already clean because of the word which I have spoken to you. Abide in Me, and I in you. As the branch cannot bear fruit of itself, unless it abides in the vine, neither can you, unless you abide in Me. I am the vine, you are the branches. He who abides in Me, and I in him, bears much fruit; for without Me you can do nothing. If anyone does not abide in Me, he is cast out as a branch and is withered; and they gather them and throw them into the fire, and they are burned. If you abide in Me, and My words abide in you, you will ask what you desire, and it shall be done for you. By this My Father is glorified, that you bear much fruit; so you will be My disciples."

—JOHN 15:1-8 (NKJV)

When He talked about abiding in His Word, it meant to dwell in it. In other words, *meditation.* When we memorize and meditate on the Word of God, we grow. The scripture likens this to a baby desiring milk for nourishment. We need the Word. We need the instructions, the principles, and the laws of the Word. We need its power.

The Bible is a powerful book. The writer of the Book of Hebrews put it this way:

> *"For the word of God is living and powerful, and sharper than any two-edged sword, piercing even to the division of soul and spirit, and of joints and marrow, and is a discerner of the thoughts and intents of the heart."*
>
> —HEBREWS 4:12 (NKJV)

And consider what the Scriptures themselves say about meditation:

> *"Keep this Book of the Law always on your lips; meditate on it day and night, so that you may be careful to do everything written in it. Then you will be prosperous and successful."*
>
> — JOSHUA 1:8

> *"How can a young person stay on the path of purity? By living according to your word. I seek you with all my heart; do not let me stray from your commands. I have hidden your word in my heart that I might not sin against you."*
>
> — PSALM 119:9-11

> *"Let the word of Christ dwell in you richly in all wisdom, teaching and admonishing one another in psalms and hymns*

*and spiritual songs, singing with grace in your hearts to the
Lord."*

— COLOSSIANS 3:16 (NKJV)

The key to meditating on Scripture is to *memorize*
Scripture. Start with verses that speak to your heart in a
personal and profound way—your "go to" verses, passages to
think of in crucial moments. Review the passage in your mind
and sort of "chew" mentally on the words. Massage them into
your brain. Turn them into a prayer and talk with God about
the Word, asking Him to make the specific truth a reality in
your life. You'll find that when you approach the Word like
this, the words will stay with you and be there for you when
you need them.

The late Dallas Willard was a prolific writer on the
subject of *spiritual formation.*

Willard had this about memorizing Scripture:

*"Bible memorization is absolutely fundamental to spiritual
formation. If I had to choose between all the disciplines of the
spiritual life, I would choose Bible memorization, because it is
a fundamental way of filling our minds with what it needs.
This Book of the Law shall not depart out of your mouth.
That's where you need it! How does it get in your mouth?
Memorization.[3]*

Think of it this way—the more Scripture you squirrel
away in your mind during normal times, the greater your

capacity to apply profound truth at decisive moments. That's soul growth.

THREE

"Woe is Me"

One of the biggest problems we face in our day and age is that most people have a severely distorted view of Jesus. And with that as a starting point, any journey is doomed to failure. It's like simple arithmetic. If you get the most basic equation wrong, it just gets worse exponentially. Thinking two plus two equals five may seem like a small mistake, but when you start a series of equations on that false foundation, after several "generations" you can be off by a factor of millions.

The main reason so many people have a distorted view of Jesus is, of course, the fact that we are all sinners. This fact is confirmed by scripture (Romans 3:23 and 3:10, etc.) as well as our behavior. In fact, every newspaper in America testifies to the sad fact of human sinfulness each morning.

And sin separates people from Almighty God.

"But your iniquities have separated you from your God; And your sins have hidden His face from you, So that He will not hear."

—ISAIAH 59:2 (NKJV)

God is transcendent and distant from us. That means our "spiritual equation" starts with a gap, with people searching for meaning and fulfillment in all the wrong places.

A famous mathematician and philosopher named Blaise Pascal said something directly on point back in the 17th century: *"There is a God-shaped vacuum in the heart of each man which cannot be satisfied by any created thing but only by God the Creator, made known through Jesus Christ."*

What he said still rings true more than 400 years later.

Too many people are on a journey to "find" a soul challenge. This is the basis for much of the educational system, both formal and informal. Go to your local bookstore and you will find a very large section dedicated to something called, "Self-Help." There will be books about everything from diet, to psychology, to relationships, and so much more.

But not one of the books actually identifies the most basic problem every human being faces—the gap between people and their creator. And when people do think about

Jesus, they superimpose their own bias on Him. He's a "Superstar," or He's all about a political movement, or He's some kind of cosmic Santa Claus.

To some, Jesus is just a "prophet," a mistake many made when He ministered on earth 2000 years ago. They miss the fact that Jesus is King of Kings and Lord of Lords. They think he was an average preacher who taught good things.

When we belittle his deity, as so many did in His day, we cut off our understanding of God. We can't get to God without Jesus (John 14:6), and that leads to so many other distortions in life.

We need to take a cue from the prophet Isaiah.

In the year that King Uzziah died, I saw the Lord sitting on a throne, high and lifted up, and the train of His robe filled the temple. Above it stood seraphim; each one had six wings: with two he covered his face, with two he covered his feet, and with two he flew. And one cried to another and said:

"Holy, holy, holy is the Lord of hosts; The whole earth is full of His glory!" And the posts of the door were shaken by the voice of him who cried out, and the house was filled with smoke.

So I said:

"Woe is me, for I am undone! Because I am a man of unclean lips, And I dwell in the midst of a people of unclean lips; For my eyes have seen the King, The Lord of hosts."

—ISAIAH 6:1-5 (NKJV)

His response to seeing God was, *"Woe is me."* It was a humbling experience, and it was an experience that helped him see himself clearly. Only when we see the greatness of God do we really see ourselves.

There is a great verse about old King Saul who was the king of Israel before David. He was the People's Choice, the king the people wanted. Saul started out strong, but his power went to his head, his ego got out of control, and he began to cross lines and do things contrary to God.

> *"And Samuel said, When thou wast little in thine own sight, wast thou not made the head of the tribes of Israel, and the Lord anointed thee king over Israel?"*
>
> —I SAMUEL 15:17

The preacher Samuel said, *"God is done with you; he is going to choose another king to replace you. You were okay when you were little in your own eyes. When you stopped being little in your own eyes, trouble happened."*

When God is big, you will always seem little in your own eyes. That is the basis of humility. So when you are down, look up. Get your eyes on God, not on yourself, not on your problems. In the Book of Hebrews there is a passage that talks about running a race and looking unto Jesus:

> *Therefore we also, since we are surrounded by so great a cloud of witnesses, let us lay aside every weight, and the sin which*

18

so easily ensnares us, and let us run with endurance the race
that is set before us, looking unto Jesus, the [a]author and
finisher of our faith, who for the joy that was set before Him
endured the cross, despising the shame, and has sat down at
the right hand of the throne of God. For consider Him who
endured such hostility from sinners against Himself, lest you
become weary and discouraged in your souls.

—HEBREWS 12:1-3 (NKJV)

We must never lose sight of the big picture, which is God and his greatness. It's all a matter of perspective. The higher our view of God, the lower our view of ourselves. It really is as simple as that.

Discovering this truth was a breakthrough moment for Simon Peter:

When Jesus came into the region of Caesarea Philippi, He
asked His disciples, saying, "Who do men say that I, the Son
of Man, am?" So they said, "Some say John the Baptist, some
Elijah, and others Jeremiah or one of the prophets." He said to
them, "But who do you say that I am?"

Simon Peter answered and said, "You are the Christ, the
Son of the living God." Jesus answered and said to him,
"Blessed are you, Simon Bar-Jonah, for flesh and blood has not
revealed this to you, but My Father who is in heaven. And I
also say to you that you are Peter, and on this rock I will build
My church, and the gates of Hades shall not prevail against
it.

—MATTHEW 16:13-18 (NKJV)

We need that kind of clarity. It's a vital part of our soul challenge, and it can only come when we make a commitment to see God through His Word.

FOUR

"From Glory to Glory"

> "So then, my beloved brethren, let every man be swift to hear, slow to speak, slow to wrath."
>
> —JAMES 1:19 (NKJV)

Sanctification is how we grow spiritually. We are not what we used to be because God is at work sanctifying us. But it is a partnership. There is His part—and ours. And for this to work, we must be teachable. That's what James is talking about when he refers to being

"swift to hear" and "slow to speak." I'm sure your mother or grandmother may have told you, "You have two ears and one mouth, so listen more than you talk."

That's wisdom.

Being teachable means you're quick to listen, especially when the Word of God is being taught. You're not pushing back against what you hear. You're not trying to find fault with the teacher or preacher. You're not arguing in your head, "But…". Frankly, too many believers aren't growing because they have too many "buts."

When teaching is going on, we should drop whatever we're doing. We should get rid of anything that distracts us. Clear your mind. We should be like Samuel after he went to Eli because he was hearing a voice from God. Like him, we should say, "Speak, Lord, for thy servant heareth."

Teachable means to be swift to hear.

But it also means I need to be slow to speak. Too many people don't grow properly because when God is trying to teach them something, they are quick to speak. They talk back to God, or right past Him. We need to learn to button our lip when God is speaking through His servants. Get quiet and listen. Our parents tried to teach us that.

We also need to learn to control our emotions in the soul growth process. We must be "slow to wrath." Watch the anger, because our wrath is incompatible with the

righteousness of God. When we are angry and grumble and complain, it short-circuits the power of God in our lives.

When we are not in control of our temper and let anger take over our heart, we cannot grow. We cannot be sanctified. The enemy will use your anger against you, even if you feel justified in it.

> Therefore lay aside all filthiness and overflow of wickedness, and receive with meekness the implanted word, which is able to save your souls. But be doers of the word, and not hearers only, deceiving yourselves. For if anyone is a hearer of the word and not a doer, he is like a man observing his natural face in a mirror; for he observes himself, goes away, and immediately forgets what kind of man he was. But he who looks into the perfect law of liberty and continues in it, and is not a forgetful hearer but a doer of the work, this one will be blessed in what he does.
>
> —JAMES 1:21-25 (NKJV)

But, while hearing may be an important place to start, it is a horrible place to stop.

People who hear the word but do nothing about it, are, according to James, deceiving themselves. And this is a form of self-delusion. We must act on the word to get any real benefit from it.

Many of us sit under teaching, but do we act on what we've heard? Or do we just make excuses? *The One-Year Soul Challenge* that I'm talking about requires us to act in faith on what we hear from God through His teachers. To hear and not do is a very real form of disobedience.

James tells us that when we fail to put God's Word into action in our lives it's like

looking at our face in a mirror for a moment. The image lasts briefly, and we quickly forget what we saw. Hearing the word, but not "doing" the word, gives us a brief glimpse of our true selves, but we quickly move on.

Did you ever meet someone who was just an awful person, but they seemed

oblivious to it? People like that are clueless as to how they come across. Sometimes we say they are not "self-aware." Well, it is only when we put God's Word into practice that we become truly "self-aware." This means to really understand our faults, weaknesses, gifts, and the progress of our sanctification.

In a real sense, sanctification verifies salvation. It's the evidence of life-change. If you have been professing salvation for many years, but you haven't really changed in all that time, in the sense of becoming more conformed to the image of Christ, you should check your soul.

As the Apostle Paul said about himself in Philippians chapter three, I haven't arrived.

But I am on the right path and I making progress.

Saved and sanctified!

Now, James said that we need to look at God's perfect law and continue in it. The perfect law is all the principles of Biblical teaching. That is what changes us—staying in the word and then putting what we learn into practice by faith.

Paul wrote about this same thing to the Corinthian church:

> *"But we all, with unveiled face, beholding as in a mirror the glory of the Lord, are being transformed into the same image from glory to glory, just as by the Spirit of the Lord."*
> —II CORINTHIANS 3:18 (NKJV)

He was talking about looking at God's word and being transformed "from glory to glory." That means "ever-increasing glory." The change is brought about when the Word of God is used by the Spirit of God. But there is one more important "ingredient" needed.

Back in the day of Moses, when he was trying to lead his people to the Promised Land, you may recall how often the people failed. They complained. They got bitter. They chased after false gods. They did some pretty bad things. Yet, they had the "word," in the sense of the promises of God. So why did they fail so miserably?

Well, here's what it says in the Book of Hebrews:

> *For indeed the gospel was preached to us as well as to them;* **but the word which they heard did not profit them, not being mixed with faith in those who heard it.** *For we who*

have believed do enter that rest, as He has said: "So I swore in My wrath, they shall not enter My rest," although the works were finished from the foundation of the world.

—HEBREWS 4:2-3 (NKJV)

This passage was describing why the Exodus generation failed to enter the Promised Land. Did you catch what it says in that Hebrews passage? The word didn't do them any good because it wasn't "mixed with faith."

Faith is the final piece of the puzzle. Sanctification is inspired by the Word, empowered by His Spirit, and activated by faith.

You need all three to make it happen, and continue in soul growth.

FIVE

"Perfect—Like Him!"

What is the picture for your life? If we don't have the right image in our minds and hearts, we'll fall very short. We'll miss the best—God's plan for our lives.

As I've already shared with you, we must focus the eyes of our hearts and minds firmly on Jesus, and we must keep them there. It's like the prophet Isaiah said:

> "You will keep him in perfect peace, whose mind is stayed on You, because he trusts in You."
>
> —ISAIAH 26:3 (NKJV)

We must zero in on Jesus at all times. He must be our constant focal point. When we do this the Spirit of God, working with the Word of God and the faith evidenced by our focus, can change our lives more and more. This will help us fulfill what it says in the great wisdom book of the Old Testament:

> *"But the path of the just is as the shining light, that shineth more and more unto the perfect day."*
>
> —PROVERBS 4:18 (KJV)

As we look closely at Jesus, we see His absolute perfection. If you are like me, I get tired of looking all the time at messed up folks. I'm tired of looking to people who really can't help me. We need to study Jesus. We need to learn everything about Him. Like Paul when He told the believers at Philippi:

> *"...that I may know Him and the power of His resurrection, and the fellowship of His sufferings, being conformed to His death."*
>
> —PHILIPPIANS 3:10 (NKJV)

Do you remember some years ago when people were wearing those bracelets that had on them the letters: WWJD? That stood for the great question to ask ourselves when faced with any choice in life: "What would Jesus do?" Well, the bracelets may be out of style, but the sentiment never should. We must, by faith, cooperate with God as He conforms us to the image of His dear Son!

This image gives us the highest standard, the most lofty goal. It may seem to be far- fetched and impossible, but it's His goal for us nonetheless.

> *"Therefore you shall be perfect, just as your Father in heaven is perfect."*
>
> —MATTHEW 5:48 (NKJV)

We are to look at Him because He is perfect. And by keeping our focus on Him, which is an act of faith, we are cooperating with the Father who progressively changes us into that image. It is a well-known concept in psychology that what we intensely focus on over time moves us toward that same image.

So perfection is the goal. We are to be perfect, as the Father is perfect. He didn't say, "be messed up, as He is messed up." God forbid. But it means the more we look intensely at Jesus, the more we become like Him.

We must remember this.

Studying Matthew 5:48 helps us in our goal setting process. It gives us the right picture for our mind and heart. It is constant reminder that we are on our way. To where? We're on our way to being like Him. The Apostle John talked about this in his first epistle.

> *"Behold what manner of love the Father has bestowed on us, that we should be called children of God! Therefore the world does not know us, because it did not know Him. Beloved, now*

we are children of God; and it has not yet been revealed what
we shall be, but we know that when He is revealed, we shall
be like Him, for we shall see Him as He is. And everyone who
has this hope in Him purifies himself, just as He is pure."
—I JOHN 3:1-3 (NKJV)

The Soul Challenge is about growing to be like Him. And we are becoming more and more like Him now, but only as we focus on Him and cooperate with Him. In other words, the closer we get to Him, the more we become like Him. It's like what happens many times with people who have been married to each other for 40 or 50 years, they become more and more like each other. Have you ever noticed that?

So, to be sanctified, study the Son. Look at His ways, his tendencies, how He walked and talked. How did He handle those who hated Him? Things like that. Look at how Jesus handled storms. I urge you to watch how He grew in favor with God and man. As you set your goals, take a closer look at Him.

He wouldn't let nothing stop Him, not even the haters.

Look at how Jesus dealt with the ultimate enemy—Satan himself. When the enemy tried to attack Him, He handled it with the Word of God. This is another reason why having a rich relationship with your Bible is so vitally important. The enemy flees when we use "the sword of the Spirit."

How about "social media"—how did Jesus deal with that? They had their own version back then. The rumor mill was always running when it came to "misinformation" about Him. They didn't have an "Internet" for posting, but they managed to do damage with lies. Do you remember when His disciples came to Him and said that some people were saying He was Elijah or another of the Prophets? That was First Century social media at work.

What did Jesus do? He turned it right around and asked the disciples, "But who do you say I am?" So, studying Jesus will help you battle the vicious cycle of information flowing all around us and help you to grow in your soul challenge to be like Him.

God has given us great resources to help us with sanctification. He has placed them all around us, to help us be conformed to the image of His Son. One of them is the church. That's right—the local church is an instrument or agent given to us by God to help me think and look like Him.

*"And he gave some, apostles; and some, prophets; and some, evangelists; and some, pastors and teachers; For the **perfecting** of the saints, for the work of the ministry, for the edifying of the body of Christ: Till we all come in the unity of the faith, and of the knowledge of the Son of God, unto a perfect man, unto the measure of the stature of the fulness of Christ: That*

we henceforth be no more children, tossed to and fro, and carried about with every wind of doctrine, by the sleight of men, and cunning craftiness, whereby they lie in wait to deceive; But speaking the truth in love, may grow up into him in all things, which is the head, even Christ: From whom the whole body fitly joined together and compacted by that which every joint supplieth, according to the effectual working in the measure of every part, maketh increase of the body unto the edifying of itself in love."

—EPHESIANS 4:11-16 (KJV)

God has given all of this to us to help us grow. And when God gives us something, we should respect those gifts. Take parents, for example. They are a gift from God, and we are to honor them.

According to the passage in Ephesians chapter four, He gives us the gifts of spiritual leaders to *perfect us*, which means to prepare or equip us for the great work of serving and building up the Body of Christ. The ultimate goal is "the stature of the fullness of Christ."

And when we don't cooperate with or appreciate the leaders He has given us, we default to being "tossed to and fro" by the "winds of doctrine"—sounds a lot like the fake stuff of social media to me.

We are accountable for growing to the people He puts in our lives.

SIX

"Getting Clean and Clear"

I want to move into the next stage of the One-Year Challenge I've been telling you about. And this part has to do with getting and maintaining a clear-cut portrait of yourself—a self-portrait. I want to dissect this idea. This is a crucial part of developing the kind of goals we need to succeed. You remember that I told you earlier about soul-goals.

And as I've already established, it all starts with a good image of Jesus Christ. He's our ultimate model. He's the goal. Everything we do needs to move us toward His image so that we can be like Him.

Your friends are not your models. Your mother is not your model. Your father is not your model. Some hero or celebrity is not your model. The greatest pattern for living is the Lord Jesus Christ. Missing that point is why so many people fall short in their lives and never seem to be able to make much of themselves.

We need to see Him in all His glory and in how He handled things. This is crucial to getting and keeping an objective and unbiased picture of ourselves. And this can make us very uncomfortable. It is not an easy step. It usually involves a certain amount of emotional and mental pain.

You see, when we look at Jesus and then look at ourselves we will immediately feel a sense of disappointment. We love to look at our beauty marks, not our blotches. We don't usually linger on our flaws. We like to think we look good, even better than other people.

This is why we need a wake-up call. This is why we need to see our own ugliness. This is unavoidable if we want to grow into the kind of people God wants us to be. This is because as long as we think we are good to go and don't need to change, we will remain on the path of mediocrity—or worse, abject failure.

When you think about it, this painful change is actually a blessing. It is a blessing because it is vital for our progress. You may think of seeing your true image—your true self—as a setback, but it's not. It's actually a giant step forward. It is progress toward greatness.

And it all starts with a self-portrait.

A few years ago, Union Station in Kansas City hosted an exhibition about the human body. I think about that when I ponder the whole idea of self-awareness. The exhibit was called *A Unique Look Into Our Marvelous Machine.* The creators took it around the country and it was seen by tens of millions of people. Described as "an inspiring journey into our human body," it described our skeletal system, nervous system, muscular system, circulatory system, and respiratory system.

One doctor has this to say about the exhibition: "People are preoccupied with their bodies, but they don't know how they function. BODY WORLDS will give them access to the many miracles of the human body and help them understand their physical selves."

That exhibit at Union Station had all the human organs on display. I wanted to see that, so I visited it. They showed the heart, the intestines, and the lungs, among so many other things. But it was the display about the lungs that really grabbed my attention.

They showed a lung that had been part of a Ten-Year Plan.

What I mean by that is that the lung was one that had been on cigarettes for that long. They showed it side by side a clear and clean lung—a nonsmoking version. The lung that had been on cigarettes looked very bad. It was blackened.

This was, of course, designed to be a wakeup call. In fact, they had a box right there where you could throw your cigarettes away after you saw what smoking was doing to your lungs. It was very effective.

You see, when you get a chance to see the truth about yourself, it can be startling. It can compel you to change. But it's important for us not just to see how this principle works relating to our physical bodies and organs. We need a clear view of our inner self. We need to dig down and see our souls. Have you ever been to the dentist for something called *root canal*? Well, what I am describing could be called spiritual root canal. It's about digging deep.

And getting clean and clear.

SEVEN

"Who Can Understand the Heart?"

"The heart is deceitful above all things,
And desperately wicked;
Who can know it?
I, the Lord, search the heart, I test the mind,
Even to give every man according to his ways, According to
the fruit of his doings.

—JEREMIAH 17:9-10 (NKJV)

God used the Prophet Jeremiah to remind us about the importance of looking deep within as we try to examine ourselves. It all has to do with our hearts deceiving us. God says our hearts are deceitful above all else. So, there's really no such thing as objectivity. We are all in bondage to selfish-subjectivity.

Our hearts love to hide the truth from us—especially the truth about ourselves. Our hearts are sick, and we all know that we are not at our best when we are sick. This is one of the reasons so many people don't really want to change. Their hearts tell them they're doing fine.

But they're not.

There's an old saying about evangelism: "To get people saved, you need to get them lost, first." In other words, in our day and age we have a hard time getting people to see themselves as they really are—in God's sight. It's a form of self-delusion. And it is driven by our hearts.

Jeremiah asks, "Who can understand the heart?" And the wise man, Solomon, has this to say:

> *"For I considered all this in my heart, so that I could declare it all: that the righteous and the wise and their works are in the hand of God. People know neither love nor hatred by anything they see before them. All things come alike to all:"*
> —ECCLESIASTES 9:1-2 (NKJV)

Solomon echoes what Jeremiah say. He confirmed that everything done "under the sun" is infected with evil. We're surrounded by it—it's our common human experience.

Both Jeremiah and Solomon were describing the fact that we are often confused about the condition of our "inner self." In a very real sense, we are delusional about ourselves.

Jesus talked about the human heart and what He had to say is pretty brutal.

> *When He had called all the multitude to Himself, He said to them, "Hear Me, everyone, and understand: There is nothing that enters a man from outside which can defile him; but the things which come out of him, those are the things that defile a man. If anyone has ears to hear, let him hear!"*
>
> *When He had entered a house away from the crowd, His disciples asked Him concerning the parable. So He said to them, "Are you thus without understanding also? Do you not perceive that whatever enters a man from outside cannot defile him, because it does not enter his heart but his stomach, and is eliminated, thus purifying all foods?" And He said, "What comes out of a man, that defiles a man. For from within, out of the heart of men, proceed evil thoughts, adulteries, fornications, murders, thefts, covetousness, wickedness, deceit, lewdness, an evil eye, blasphemy, pride, foolishness. All these evil things come from within and defile a man."*
>
> — MARK 7:14-23 (NKJV)

Our Lord told us that our problems come from within, from that desperately wicked and deceitful heart. Have you ever heard the idea that people are bad because their environment is bad? Well, Jesus shoots that fairy tale theory all to pieces. He tells us that we are prone to evil from inside out, not the outside in.

Because we are ugly on the inside, we are prone to act ugly on the outside. We are capable of all sorts of bad stuff, from sexual sins, to stealing, to pride, and so forth. People do hurtful things to other people, because they are hurt and broken on the inside. Do you want to know the root cause of low self-esteem? Look no further than your heart. The heart causes some to think of themselves more highly than they ought to think. But it also causes some to think more lowly of themselves than they ought to think.

Remember that blackened lung I wrote about? Well, it's time for a wake-up call about the blackened nature of our hearts!

EIGHT

"Watch Yourself—and Learn"

"For as he thinks in his heart, so is he."
—PROVERBS 23:7 (NKJV)

God wants us to know that how we think in our hearts and minds determines our behavior—how we act and react when it comes to the world around us. So we all need help. Lots of help.

There are some proven techniques to help us. They will help you to see the real you.

But like any good therapist will tell you, we have to be willing to do the work. We must work the problem to make any real progress.

The first thing we need to do is to come to grip with our own tendencies. We need to determine how our personality leans. The Apostle Paul wrote about this to the church at Corinth, stressing the importance of self-examination.

> *"Examine yourselves as to whether you are in the faith. Test yourselves. Do you not know yourselves, that Jesus Christ is in you?—unless indeed you are disqualified."*
> —II CORINTHIANS 13:5 (NKJV)

Notice the goal was to find that "Jesus Christ is in you." That makes all the difference. We need to know our tendencies so we can know how to handle the storms that come our way. And they surely do. I'm using storms as a metaphor for those turbulent and confusing things that come our way. They are things that happen to us.

Did you know that there are people called "storm chasers"? They like to follow the weather and see things like tornados. Sounds a little crazy to me. In fact, I've never had to chase a storm.

Storms chase me.

As we examine how we handle the storms that rage through our lives, usually coming out of the blue, we can see how much we are like or unlike Jesus. We need to watch such things. They reveal a lot.

We need to watch ourselves. But we also need to watch our family dynamics, too. This is because family dynamics have a great impact on understanding ourselves and our self-esteem. Family dynamics are also key to understanding how we handle conflict. When we are attacked, how do we handle it? How do we respond? How do we handle those who try to hurt us? How do we handle our haters?

These are important questions to ask as we examine ourselves. This is something we should make a serious effort to track in our pursuit of the kind of soul goals that will bring short term and long term growth to our soul challenge.

Also, we need to look at how we handle our weaknesses. We all have them. We get fearful, we have bad habits, we give in to temptation. These are all very real problems. And they are all part of the mix as we try to get a clear portrait of ourselves for soul growth.

But, again, this is a painful process—I can never say this too much.

Do you run from trouble, or do you stand and face it? That's another great examination question. You need to discern if you have an assertive personality or if you are passive. How about this one: Do you need other people to validate what you are, what you think, or what you have done? We must be clear about these things to have a clear self-portrait of ourselves.

Watch yourself—and learn. Never look to others to find a clear picture of who you are. Paul talked about this to the church at Corinth:

*"For we dare not class ourselves or **compare** ourselves with those who commend themselves. But they, measuring themselves by themselves, and comparing themselves among themselves, are not wise."*

—II CORINTHIANS 10:12 (NKJV)

He clearly states that comparing ourselves with others is not a wise practice.

However, this does not mean that we don't need others—we do. God has ordained for you to have people in your circle who can help you get this clear picture of who you are. So don't be afraid to ask them.

And never be afraid to ask the Holy Spirit.

The Holy Spirit will always tell you the truth. He will bear witness about your identity and relationship with Christ. Paul said it this way in the Book of Romans:

"For as many as are led by the Spirit of God, these are sons of God. For you did not receive the spirit of bondage again to fear, but you received the Spirit of adoption by whom we cry out, 'Abba, Father.' The Spirit Himself bears witness with our spirit that we are children of God,"

— ROMANS 8:14-16 (NKJV)

With good teaching, the Holy Spirit will help you see who you are. We can depend on Him. We need good teaching. This teaching must be from the Word of God. Yes, this means you need a spiritual teacher who proclaims the Word. The Word of God is a mirror, as we saw earlier when we talked about James chapter one. Therefore, the Word helps us to see ourselves. Good teaching from the Word is vital.

We need the Word of God. It's the "sword" the Holy Spirit uses.

> *"Finally, my brethren, be strong in the Lord and in the power of His might. Put on the whole armor of God, that you may be able to stand against the wiles of the devil. For we do not wrestle against flesh and blood, but against principalities, against powers, against the rulers of the darkness of this age, against spiritual hosts of wickedness in the heavenly places.*
>
> *Therefore take up the whole armor of God, that you may be able to withstand in the evil day, and having done all, to stand. Stand therefore, having girded your waist with truth, having put on the breastplate of righteousness, and having shod your feet with the preparation of the gospel of peace; above all, taking the shield of faith with which you will be able to quench all the fiery darts of the wicked one. And take the helmet of salvation, and the sword of the Spirit, which is the word of God;"*
>
> —EPHESIANS 6:12-17 (NKJV)

"For the word of God is living and powerful, and sharper than any two-edged sword, piercing even to the division of soul and spirit, and of joints and marrow, and is a discerner of the thoughts and intents of the heart."

—HEBREWS 4:12 (NKJV)

According to these passages of scripture, God's Word is a tool used by the Holy Spirit. And notice in the Hebrews verse that it has a way of getting into our inner self. It does surgery on our souls. And it even understands our thoughts and motives. When we are in the Word, we benefit from the best therapy in the universe. Time spent under the teaching and preaching of God's Word is also the best *group* therapy.

But there are times we need a licensed profession. People who are trained in the workings of the human mind can help us learn about ourselves. I know that there is sometimes a stigma around this kind of therapy—especially among church folk. But sometimes we need it to help us see ourselves.

One more thing we need is to have wise and Spirit-filled Christians in our lives.

These are people who will tell us the truth about ourselves. They will be iron that sharpens iron. We need people who really know us and who will be willing to be brutally honest with us.

When we get these "techniques" working for us, our latter will be greater than our former.

NINE

"Jesus is Our Model"

"*Therefore, if anyone is in Christ, he is a new creation; old things have passed away; behold, all things have become new.*"

—II Corinthians 5:17 (NKJV)

We're talking about the construction of a new you—a brand new man or woman. But I want you to understand that the construction of the new you is not a rebuild. You are not reconstructing the old you. It is a new construction. Anyone who is in Christ is a new creation. Old things have passed away. All things have become new. You are a new construction. This is a new you. You have been put together by the power of God and with an anointing of the Holy Spirit.

When you cooperate with God's plan for you, you are becoming a totally new you—one that did not previously exist.

It doesn't matter how old you are. God is not limited by the amount of time you had been the way that you were before Christ. He has a whole life for you as a new creation.

There is still a lot that you haven't seen or comprehended that God wants to do in and through the new you. There is a lot that has not yet been brought forth.

> But as it is written: "Eye has not seen, nor ear heard, Nor have entered into the heart of man The things which God has prepared for those who love Him."
>
> —I Corinthians 2:9 (NKJV)

How do we know that? Because you are still alive. If you are still here, God is still working on you. The new you has not yet been brought into full reality. This should excite us. If you are sad, down, and disappointed, it is a lot more difficult to grow into who God made you to be. So, get excited about the things that the new you will do!

There are some things you cannot do now. But, there are other things that, as you change, you will be able to do. Get excited about doors that will open for you that you will be able to walk through. He is changing you. He does not want you to stay the same. He wants to take you to new heights. He wants to take you to new levels. He wants to bring you into a new level of peace that you have never experienced in your life. He wants to bring you into new spiritual prosperity. He wants you to reach a new spiritual status. Get excited! God wants you to anticipate the new possibilities of the new you.

As we move towards destruction, God wants you to prepare your soul for His construction work. Construction means work. There is no construction without work. So you need to prepare your soul for this work. You cannot and will not bring forth a new you without being ready for the work.

"So then, my beloved, just as you have always obeyed, not as in my presence only, but now much more in my absence, work out your own salvation with fear and trembling."
—PHILIPPIANS 2:12

You have to do the work. What work? Paul is talking about working out the new you.

Preparing your soul to work.

Our Model

As we have talked about the construction process already, we have a good picture of Jesus. We see Him for who He is. We have a clear picture of His love and power. That is why we worship Him. That is why we study Him. That's why we eat, sleep and breathe Him. We do all we can to know Jesus, because we want to have a clear picture of who He is. Why?

Because Jesus is the model.

We keep our eyes on the model. The writer of the Book of Hebrews says, *"Looking unto Jesus, the author and finisher of our faith."* He is the model for our construction. We have to keep this clear picture of Jesus in our minds. We also need to have a clear picture of who we are. We need to clearly see our tendencies, our patterns, our hurts, our struggles, our family dynamics, our problems, our sins, our strengths, and our weaknesses. We have to know who we are. You cannot proceed to the new you without understanding the old you.

We must know who we were, and know who we are now, in light of our relationship with Jesus.

I love my daughter Chelsea. I love her tremendously. A while back, I worked on a construction project for her. I guess I did a pretty good job. Even though I had been messing up quite a bit. But she kept calling me back to do more work, even though I didn't do it perfectly. She kept getting more furniture that she asked me to put together. And every time I did one of these projects, I learned something new. My skills improved. I gained experience. So thank you, Chelsea. Because of you, I have learned that construction is a *process*. If you keep doing something long enough, even though you mess up, you will eventually learn something and improve.

When we know who we are and when we look at the model of Jesus, the construction can move forward. But, there are some instructions for that construction. First, before you start, make sure you have all the *tools* you need. You must have all the pieces and parts and tools that you will use during the process. When I was doing the various building and construction work for my daughter, one thing that I noticed was the first page of the directions on every manual and instruction page for putting something together. The first page always listed and labeled the parts. I had to make sure I had all the parts, and I needed to know what each part was. So when it called for part C-1, I would know which one to grab.

Have you ever tried to use a wrong part when putting something together? It does not end well, for the project or for you. The manufacturer knows this, so the pieces are labeled. The manufacturer wants us to be successful.

And so it is with your soul construction to become like Jesus. We must label all the parts that we need help with. We need to know what His love is and be able to recognize it in our lives. I am so thankful that Jesus has love for us that is unconditional. But we need to know that, and recognize what it looks like. We need to know that His love is always there.

We need to label and know His forgiveness. How many of us have messed up? But when we know His forgiveness, we know that it is ours, because by His stripes we have been healed and forgiven. We have been cleaned up.

We need to know His grace, and what it does for us when we fall down and make mistakes on our journey. And you better believe that later in the construction process, you will need His grace. Our journey will require some grace. It is the same with mercy. We will need His mercy on this journey, because none of us are perfect.

We will need His power.

We need to know the parts that are needed, before we even start. We have to understand what they are and what role they play in our lives, so that they are at the ready when we need them. So, I noticed that in every construction project, the manual first wants you to know the pieces that you will be using. But next, you need to know the tools that you would need. You're going to need a hammer. You will need a drill. And whatever other tools it calls for.

Before trying to move too fast, without checking on these items, you need to slow yourself down, or you will not be able to complete the project. You must have the tools readily available for your new construction. So, in your own soul construction, what tools do you require?

You need the Word of God. It is a fact that you cannot be the best you without the Word of God. You need your spiritual advisors. We talked about that. Don't try to do it alone. God has put people in your life that you are going to need. So identify those people ahead of time. Who will you turn to for help when you get stuck? You need your tools at the ready.

TEN

"Enjoy!"

The second thing for this ultimate construction project is to keep the model near us. Keep the picture of the model close near you and in your heart, mind and soul. As I did projects for my daughter, I noticed that I frequently had to look at the picture. I had to compare what I was doing to the picture in the instruction manual. So I kept that picture with me. Why did I need to keep the picture near me? So as I am building and constructing I can constantly refer back to the perfect model. I can see with my eyes what it is supposed to look like.

As God is shaping the new you, producing the new you, you need to always have Jesus. He should always be close in your sight and in the forefront of your mind. But so often we lay the model aside. We don't look to Jesus first. But thank

God, we can go farther in life when we keep our eyes on Jesus. Isaiah 26:3 tells us that He will keep you in peace, if your mind is stayed on Him and if you trust Him. You have to keep your mind on the Lord for the construction process.

As I was doing the work for my daughter, I realized I was constantly referring back to the model. Because if I kept a clear picture of what the model looked like, I can stay on track to successfully build it correctly. But in life, so many times we go off kilter because we don't remember the model. We don't look to the model for direction. We don't keep the model close enough for complex decisions.

So we must keep Jesus close. We must constantly look to Him and refer to Him and His life. How would Jesus do this? What does Jesus look like in this situation? Always keep the model near you.

The third thing we need is simply to *enjoy the process*. That's right. Enjoy the process. The tendency many of us have may be to get weary during the construction. Change is hard.

Growth is uncomfortable. It is going to be a long, sometimes tedious process. Constructing a whole new you is going to be a long project. In fact, it is going to be a lifelong process. You must learn to enjoy the journey. You are going to have some good days. You are going to have some bad days.

But we must learn to have joy in the process of the construction of our new selves.

How do you do this? You have to learn how to relax. You have to learn how to stay calm through the complexities of the construction. You must thank God through each season. We can never learn how to be our best selves if we are constantly frantic, irritated and out of control. We must ask God to show us how to enjoy our soul growth process.

Go, eat your bread with joy,

   And drink your wine with a merry heart; For God has already accepted your works.

   Let your garments always be white, And let your head lack no oil.

   Live joyfully with the wife whom you love all the days of your vain life which He has given you under the sun, all your days of vanity; for that is your portion in life, and in the labor which you perform under the sun.

—ECCLESIASTES 9:7-9 (NKJV)

Enjoy yourself. Why get all worked up when things don't go your way? Have a good time.

Choose humor and joy! Surround yourself with those who will help you enjoy life. If you're around people and they are constantly bringing you down and making you uptight, then you had better go back to the instructions. Because in order to produce the new you, you've got to have a state of calmness and enjoy the process because it's going to be a tedious and long journey. Jesus kept people around Him to help Him with the goals of His Father's mission for His life.

So when doing projects for my daughter, I would put some music on and enjoy the atmosphere, so I could put together the project with a joyous spirit. And we can do the same to help us in our soul construction.

The fourth thing to remember for our construction project is to *expect to make some mistakes.* Remember, only the model is perfect. The model has no flaws. But you are imperfect. You have flaws and you will make mistakes. So as you look at yourself, and refer to the model, you will see where you are different. This is natural. It is going to happen. But don't stay there. Don't stop there.

When I was constructing the projects, I noticed that I made some mistakes—some big and some small. But I didn't stop building. I didn't throw a pity party. I got myself back up, looked at the instructions and kept moving forward.

In our lives, we can thank God through these seasons. We can learn from our mistakes and our mess ups. This is because in our soul challenge we grow as a result of our downfalls. We must learn how to keep on moving forward. Because as long as you are moving forward, you are moving to the better you. So, you have to learn and understand that making mistakes is a part of your construction journey.

How many of you have made mistakes in your life? Have you made mistakes this year? Look back and see what you did, how you fell, what mistakes you made. But, I'm sure you can also look back and see your progress. You can see how God has brought you out from those mistakes and set you on the right construction soul path.

In doing construction, I learned to avoid doing the things that caused me to make mistakes previously. So, I corrected and redirected my mistakes. If you learn the lesson from your mistakes, you can save yourself heartache and pain in the future.

The fifth thing to bear in mind during construction is to resist the temptation to cheat. What do I mean by that? When I was working on these projects, I noticed that I would get tempted to not pick up the instructions and just wing it on my own. Once I saw good progress, I would think that I could skip steps. I would say in my head, "I got this." "I don't need the help." So I would ignore the instructions.

Of course, that never ends well. I would find out later that I had put C-1 in D-5 and now the whole thing was off. Then I had to tear the whole thing back apart—all because I tried to cheat. And in life, you can't cheat the process. So we must resist the temptation to cheat. We can't look for shortcuts. It's a trap. You need the Word of God. You need the help of others to support you. And you must resist that voice that tells you that you can do it on your own. As you are getting on your feet, as you are progressing, as you are prospering, as God is blessing your soul, don't fall into the trap of thinking that you can do it without all the spiritual tools He has given you. Don't fall into the trap of thinking that you can do it without what The Word says. Don't think you can do it without sticking to the Model! Resist those thoughts.

Resist that temptation.

If you don't resist that temptation you will find out that you are building it all wrong, even when you thought you had it right. Pride comes before the fall. And when you begin to think that you don't need God, that you don't need the Word, that you don't need to be faithful to the teachings of the Bible, what you are really saying is that you can wing it without God.

Life is too important and short to wing it. You don't want to try to make it up as you go. You don't want to just feel your way through it and hope for the best. God has given us a blueprint. We should thank Him every day for that blueprint. He gives us a map with directions on how to get to where we are going. The Bible has everything that we need to know about life. How to raise our children. How to deal with sickness. How to make it through struggles and storms. How to make it when we have money. How to make it when we don't have money.

It's all in the soul growth instructions.

ELEVEN

"For the New You"

"Not that I have already attained, or am already perfected;
but I press on, that I may lay hold of that for which Christ
Jesus has also laid hold of me."

—PHILIPPIANS 3:12 (NKJV)

The sixth thing we need to keep in mind is this—when you get stuck, go back to the instructions. When I was doing those construction projects, I often noticed that I would start the project, and it would be going along nicely, but then I would eventually come to a certain point where I didn't understand where I was, or what my next step was.

My first tendency was to think that the manufacturer had made a mistake or had given me the wrong parts. They had gotten the instructions wrong. I had read the instructions several times, and it wasn't making sense. I could not move forward with any comprehension. So I would go back to the instructions. Again, I didn't just wing it, assuming the instructions were wrong. I had to trust the instructions and look more closely at what they were telling me to do, even if I had to backtrack a bit.

In our spiritual construction journey, we must always go back and look more carefully at the instructions when we are confused and perplexed. If you believe that the Bible is right, and you trust God's Word because you know and trust Jesus, then, logically, the misunderstanding falls on you—not God. His ways are perfect. Even if we don't understand it, we have to trust it.

Sometimes God's ways do not make sense to our human minds. We can't see the big picture. We feel stuck. We can't fully comprehend what He is doing in us. But trust Him, and go back to the instructions. The instructions are consistent, even when our thoughts and feelings are not. When you don't understand, get down on your knees and ask the Lord to help you to get it—to understand it. And don't move forward until you understand the instruction. Don't wing it on your own. And then, even if you don't understand, follow what He says to do.

For example, love those who spitefully misuse you. That command does not make sense, but we must do it anyway. There's nothing wrong with the instructions. And when we follow them in faith, we often get the understanding after we obey. When we deviate from the instructions because we don't understand, we often make a mess of things. When you get stuck, stay there. Ask God to help you to understand, because nothing is wrong with the instructions. The only thing that is wrong is your comprehension of, and obedience to, the instructions.

The seventh crucial thing is to remember there will be some parts in the instructions that will require you to ask for assistance from a spiritual partner. You will come to a step in the process that says you can't do this part without another person.

On one of my projects, I saw that it would be beneficial to have another person to help me, but I decided to wing it by myself. And for a while I thought I was doing great. And then the whole thing collapsed. God has given you spiritual partners, spiritual advisors and spiritual mentors. So stop trying to do it on your own. You have intimate friendships that God has given you, and you need to lean on them for certain steps of the journey. You will need a shoulder to cry on. You will need someone to hold you up. You will need someone to hold a piece up while you get it connected.

Thank God that whatever you need, He will provide. So get some help when you need it. You don't have to do it alone. That's not God's plan for you. Don't try to be a macho man and carry all of the burden yourself. By God's design, there are parts of the plan that require a partner or partners. Everyone needs someone to walk with them as they conquer difficult endeavors. Even superheroes have trusty sidekicks that help them. God will send you those people who will help you on your journey.

I had to learn that in the construction process—when you see that you've gotten something all wrong, it's ok to start over. Don't be afraid to tear it up and begin again. If through the process you have built something on a shaky foundation, you may have to start again at the beginning. If you constructed your marriage on bad principles. If you constructed your career on a shaky foundation. Be honest with yourself and don't be afraid to address the issues and start over. Yes, it's tedious. Yes, you have to tear some things down before you rebuild, and it can get messy. But God has grace for us and loves building new things, and you will be better off in the end.

That is what Jeremiah was shown when God took him to the Potter's house. God showed Jeremiah the clay in the hands of the Potter, and the Potter remade it again. We can thank God that when we mess up, He wants to remake us over again, even in the middle of the construction process. We can always start over. And that is worth giving God praise and thanks. In the process of construction, the instructions allow God to produce a new you.

And you'd better get ready for it. Get ready for the new doors that will be opened for you.

Are you ready for the challenge?

Endnotes

[1] Genesis 3:19

[2] II Corinthians 10:12

[3] *Spiritual Formation in Christ for the Whole Life and Whole Person*, in "Vocatio," Vol. 12, no. 2, Spring, 2001